COME TO GOD'S TABLE

Preparing for Holy Communion

STANLEY N. OLSON

Augsburg Fortress, Minneapolis

Table of contents

Come to God's Table

This leader guide is accompanied by a communicant book and a parent book.

Susan Niemi Tetlie and Sandra Paulson-Nemzek, editors
Lecy design, cover and text design
Photographers: Mimi Forsyth, pages 3, 6. William Zuehlke, 11. Jean-Claude Lejeune, 15, 18, 21. Marilyn Nolt, 24, 27. CLEO, 29, 48, 50. Skjold Photographs, 32, 34. Dave Anderson, 38, 41, 43.

Manufactured in U.S.A.

4 5 6 7 8 9

Introduction

Come to God's Table is designed to help children and their parents prepare for Holy Communion. Most of the children using this resource will be approaching their first participation in the Lord's Supper. However, the material can be used to deepen the understanding and interest of children who are already participating in the sacrament. We all need to prepare for Holy Communion—the first time and every time.

Most congregations prepare children for Communion in the fifth grade. Therefore, this material is aimed at the upper elementary child—age nine to eleven. These are good years for learning more about this sacrament. Holy

Communion centers on the physical, or earthly, elements of bread and wine and these can be experienced and appreciated as gifts of love, even by the young. However, the fifth grader can likely explore the broader implications of that love for service and community. Adults can have a fresh look at familiar truths through the eyes of these children who are growing in many ways.

Partners in learning

Come to God's Table encourages a partnership in learning among the children, their parents and other adults, and the teachers and pastors who represent the congregation.

The upper elementary student

Upper elementary students share important characteristics as they move toward adolescence. Development does not take place at an even rate in all children, but general traits can be noted.

Tasks challenge these children and they want to develop skills. There is a strong need for feelings of accomplishment and individual competence. The students are still motivated by the wish to please their teacher, and leaders will need to recognize and praise growth. Teaching methods should build on this need to master tasks and information. Learning activities should not always focus on responding to the teacher, but should give children an opportunity to make their own discoveries and raise their own questions. Movement and physical involvement in learning are useful.

Peer involvement is very important for upper elementary children. They need the recognition of the group. They need a sense of place and belonging, even if it comes only by being the class clown. Boys and girls are discovering more of their sexuality, and peer acceptance includes doing what is expected of one as a boy or a girl. This course may provide opportunities for encouraging qualities like acceptance, forgiveness, service, and gentleness, which contribute to positive experiences of belonging.

Upper elementary students still think very concretely although they are developing their abilities to classify and

relate pieces of information and draw generalizations. Teachers will see both abstract and concrete thinking in the same child and considerable diversity within a group. For example, God is thought of as friend or parent but there is a growing awareness that God cannot be as physically limited as those terms imply. However, consistent abstract thinking comes later, usually about age 13, and fifth graders may have difficulty with the concept of God as spirit, which could help solve the abstract problem they recognize.

Students at this age develop their faith by identifying with the Christian community. They will be interested to know what the church believes—though it must be expressed in ways they can comprehend. The Small Catechism and Bible are useful tools in sharing the common faith. The teacher's thoughts are also of great interest to these children, and what you say will be given consideration and scrutiny. They will recognize and appreciate sincerity, consistency, and humor.

In tension with this interest in the community's faith is the desire of these children to reconcile their own understanding and experiences with what they learn of the inherited faith. For example, they may sense the problem of evil in God's world or feel some tension between their scientific knowledge and what they think the church teaches about the natural world. Though they do not yet have the reasoning ability to resolve many of their questions, they are working on them.

"What do you think?" is often a good response to a question a child raises. Children need a forum for expressing their questions and doubts. Offering a comfortable opportunity to talk about these is more important than providing precise answers. Be a well-informed guide who will help the students a few steps along the way to a mature faith.

Be sensitive to the different growth patterns that each child experiences. It is likely that you will have at least one child whose academic or emotional development lags behind the others. Many children with learning disabilities need help with reading and writing activities. By modifying a task, working in groups, giving partial answers or clues, and offering extra help, you can allow these children to participate more fully in session activities. Respond positively to each child's strengths and let the students know that they are valuable class members.

The role of the leader

The teacher or leader of this course is invited to share the good news with the young people and their families. Keep the emphasis on telling the news rather than on testing knowledge or commitment. Luther's Small Catechism reminds us that right preparation for Holy Communion is not knowledge, but belief. Trust is the primary objective. And understanding is a good means to nourish trust.

For that reason, *Come to God's Table* contains considerable information and stresses understanding because

10-year-olds are eager for knowledge. Leaders will want to use and modify material to help their students better understand the background and significance of Holy Communion. This short course cannot possibly cover all that the church knows about the Lord's Supper—not even all that could be understood by upper elementary children. Picture yourself as one teacher in a succession of many who will lead these people toward better understanding.

Finally, remember that the sacrament itself is God's gift for deepening faith. Prepared participation in the Lord's Supper will keep these children and their families growing in faith and understanding. Your role is to help each one hear God's gracious promise a little more clearly.

The role of the parent or adult

In helping a child prepare for Holy Communion, the role of parent may be filled by someone other than the child's own parent. In consultation with the pastor, leaders should be sure that each young person will be linked with an adult who is willing and able to be involved. If a parent cannot or will not fulfill this role, possible persons to ask are other relatives, baptismal sponsors, and present or former Sunday school teachers. Normally the leader should not try to fulfill this function for a child. Throughout the material, references to parents should be understood as referring to all adults filling that role. If you have adults involved who are not the parents, be sure to refer to adults rather than parents when giving instructions.

Most classes will include children with a variety of parental situations—married parents, single parents, divorced parents still involved in parenting. Normally, all parents should be invited to be involved and made to feel welcome and important. Telephoning is a good supplement to letters. You might recruit a few parents to assist you with this.

The parent role, like that of the leader, should focus on graciously sharing the good news of God's love. Encourage this approach both during the sessions and at home.

Planning the course

These materials are designed for five sessions, and include a session for parents only. Parental presence (or that of another adult) is important at the first and last sessions, and is an option throughout. The session for parents only may be taught following Session 1 or at another time that is convenient.

Format options

Each session is intended to last 50-60 minutes though suggestions are given to lengthen the sessions. Keep in mind the limited attention span of children this age. It is essential to plan for variety.

Several formats are possible for using the material. It is important that parents be present for at least three sessions (first, parents only, and last). Following are some suggestions for using the course.

- ▶ A five-week series meeting at the same time each week.
- ▶ A series where the sessions with parents are held on evenings and intervening sessions are held after school or at some other appropriate time.
- ▶ Three longer time blocks (Saturday mornings, Sunday evenings, etc.) combining Session 1 and the session for parents, Sessions 2 and 3, and Sessions 4 and 5.
- ▶ A week of day camp or vacation Bible school (with parents!).

The congregation's pastor should be directly involved in planning this course. It is important that the pastor be present at least for the first and last sessions and the parents' session. If various leaders will be used for different sessions, coordination and commitment to planned objectives is essential.

If Holy Communion is infrequent in your congregation, schedule this course so that Communion will be celebrated shortly after the final session.

The resources

The communicant book is written for the child's use during sessions and as a resource to be taken home when the course is completed. It is divided into five sessions, each following the same format. Four take-home leaflets are stapled into the center of the communicant book. They are to be removed in advance by the leader. Projects in each leaflet are designed to be used either during the session or independently at home. The last page of each leaflet asks the student to gather some data and use it for leading home devotions.

The parent book is designed to complement the course by providing information for reviewing the meaning of Holy Communion. It also answers a number of frequently asked questions and provides a glossary.

The leader guide will assist those planning and leading the course. It suggests learning objectives and offers help for using these resources, The Small Catechism, and the Bible.

The videotape *At the Lord's Table* (available from Augsburg Fortress) is an excellent additional resource. The first segment is 15 minutes long. It begins with Baptism and explores the meaning of the sacrament with the following eight statements.

Holy Communion is:

- remembering
- eating and drinking
- receiving forgiveness
- giving thanks
- celebrating
- being together
- looking to the future
- being strengthened to serve God

Use of this portion of the videotape is suggested as an optional introduction in Session 1 and as a optional review in Session 5.

The final five minutes of the videotape add a video glossary that explains names for the sacrament: Lord's Supper, Holy Communion, Sacrament of the Altar, Eucharist. It also discusses aspects and forms of distributing

the sacrament: loaf, wafer, chalice, individual glasses, pouring chalice, intinction.

Planning a session

Pastors and others who teach these Holy Communion classes often have only limited experience teaching children this age. A 10-year-old child's ways of thinking and learning are quite different from those of an adult or even of a young teenager. (Be sure to read "The Upper Elementary Student" on page 5 to review age-level characteristics.)

To assist the leader with limited experience, detailed suggestions are given for leading each session. Each session involving the students follows the same format. Following are the parts of each session.

Overview. A brief statement on the content of the session.

Objectives. These objectives identify ways to focus your teaching.

Materials needed. This is a list of items needed to teach the session.

Session background. Helpful suggestions to prepare for teaching the session.

Before the session. A list of what you need to do before class.

SESSION PLAN

Opening. An activity to begin the session.

Learning the main ideas. Suggestions for using the communicant book and teaching the content.

Reinforcing the learning. Suggestions for activities to reinforce and review the learning.

Challenges and options. Ways to lengthen the session using additional activities.

Closing. An activity and suggestions for ending the session.

Since the resources suggest more than enough material for each session, you will need to make choices according to your special concerns and the needs of your students. Make choices according to what you want to accomplish. For each session, objectives are to guide you through the session. These objectives maintain a balance among cognitive, affective, and action-oriented learning. As you make choices, keep a balance in mind. Avoid the temptation to concentrate on cognitive objectives—teach them the facts! That approach is usually counterproductive, especially with children. Young people learn best in the broad context of their lives.

"Plan carefully" and "be flexible" are both good mottos for teachers of upper elementary children. Because of their energy level, the leader must know exactly what he or she wants to accomplish and what the students will be doing. All information and materials must be ready. Flexibility is important because some of the best learning can take place by following a spontaneous idea or unexpected question. Also, parts of your session plan may take more or less time than you anticipated. Be flexible about what you do, but keep the objectives firmly in mind.

Session 1: A meal celebrating God's love

Overview

This session focuses on the love of God that underlies all aspects of Christian life and creates our trust in God. The Holy Communion meal is one of the means of grace, along with Baptism and the Word.

Objectives

This session will help children:

- understand the importance of grace in Holy Communion and the variety of meanings that surround it;
- appreciate God's use of physical elements and words of promise in the sacraments;
- share questions and observations about Holy Communion.

This session will help parents:

- remember the emphasis on grace and physical elements in the sacraments;
- appreciate the possibility of finding new meanings in Holy Communion;
- begin or continue a conversation with the child about the meaning of Holy Communion.

Materials needed

- *General materials:* communicant books, leaflets for Session 1, pencils, Bibles, chalkboard and chalk or newsprint and markers

- *Welcome:* name tags (optional)
- *Reinforcing the learning:* videotape *At the Lord's Table* and equipment for showing the video (optional)
- *Closing:* cards or half sheets of paper

Session background

The people of Israel discovered the forgiving mercy of God. Paul the apostle realized God's love is for all people. Martin Luther's life was transformed by the certainty that God is gracious. God's people today continue to experience the renewing power of that love. When we speak of the love of God, we are not referring merely to an attitude or emotion. God's love is active and effective. It changes human lives by justifying, restoring, renewing, and forgiving.

Holy Communion is one of the means through which Christians know God's love and experience its transforming effects. Lutherans call the Word, Holy Baptism, and Holy Communion *means of grace* because of God's promise to bless us through them. The latter two we call *sacraments* to designate them as ceremonies that were commanded by our Lord and use physical elements to make God's love real.

One of the doctrinal disputes about Holy Communion has to do with its essential direction. Is it our response to God or God's coming to us? Lutherans insist that Holy Communion is God coming to us. Of course, a celebration of the love of God will include our thankfulness, but God's action is always primary. God's love creates the response of thanksgiving.

Before the session

Study the list of children and adults likely to attend so that you know their names.

Read through all three resources (communicant book, parent book, and leader guide) to become familiar with the contents.

Consider the suggested objectives for this session and select the materials and activities that will help you achieve them.

Sharing refreshments after the session provides a good conversation time. If you wish to do this, make necessary arrangements.

Have materials ready for the session. Remove all four leaflets from each communicant book. Prepare name tags if there is any possibility that some in the group will not know everyone.

Preview the video if you plan to use it. (See "The Resources" on page 10 of this guide.)

Practice reading the story on page 4 of the communicant book or give one of the parents a chance to practice it.

If you will be continuing with a brief parents' session after the joint session, arrange for supervision of the children.

SESSION PLAN

Welcome

Be in the meeting area well in advance. Greet people as they arrive, learning any names you don't know. Be sure to be friendly. Pay special attention to the children. Greet them individually with a smile and a word of welcome, using their names if possible. Distribute name tags if you've decided to use them. (Be sure to wear one yourself.)

Ask parents to sit with their young person. If any child arrives without an adult, quietly team up that person with another parent.

Opening

When it's time to begin, welcome the whole group and open by reading John 3:16-17. Use the following prayer or one of your own.

Our gracious God, we thank you for the love that sent Jesus to the world. Help us as young people and adults to learn how that love is made real for us in Holy Communion. Amen.

Tell the group this first session will focus on the most important thing to know about God. Ask them, beginning with the children, what they think is the most important thing. Accept all answers, but keep asking for more until someone mentions God's love. Explain that you will all be thinking together about God's love and especially about receiving God's love in Holy Communion.

You may have some young people in the group who have already begun to receive Communion. If there is any possibility of that, be sure to mention that these sessions are a time to learn more about the Lord's Supper—whether one has not yet begun to receive it or has been receiving for a short time or a long time.

Learning the main ideas

Distribute the communicant books to the children. Tell the group that the book will help them explore God's love as we receive it in the Lord's Supper. Invite them to page through the book for a moment and then turn to the story "The Truth about the Bread and Wine" on page 4.

You or one of the other adults should read the whole story in a lively voice. Ask questions such as: What kinds of things did Joshua notice during Communion services? What did Pastor Maria say to children who didn't receive Communion? Do you think it's true that God loves you? What does the story tell you about Holy Communion? Listen for an answer that links Holy Communion with God's love and then emphasize that point.

Have parent and child together read "Focus" on page 5 of the communicant book. They should discuss the questions and write down the answers on which they agree.

God's attitude toward our world is love.

Holy Communion is a celebration of God's love; the bread and wine convince us of God's love.

If a blessing is given to noncommuning children in your congregation, ask the children if they remember what is said. Invite opinions as to why those particular words are used. If it is not done in your congregation, ask if anyone has experienced it elsewhere.

Invite the group to decide what they would say to noncommuning children if they were the pastor. You may be able to pursue some suggestions by asking for their reasons.

To introduce "Get the Point" on page 5 of the communicant book, ask, "Do you remember when and how you became part of God's family?" Guide the group, if necessary, to think of their Baptism. Ask for volunteers to tell where they were baptized and at what age. Tell them that every Baptism is evidence of God's love.

Ask children and adult volunteers to take turns reading this section aloud. Be ready to assist with any problem words. Ask the children to summarize the meaning of this section or some of the more important paragraphs (the first paragraph and the last two paragraphs). Ask each child/adult team to name one instance in life where words and a physical thing are combined to convince someone of love. Invite sharing.

For review, ask the group to name ceremonies or customs in worship that combine physical things with words to help us know God's love. *(Holy Baptism and Holy Communion.)* You'll likely get other answers such as sharing the peace or the offering. Accept all ideas but point out that Baptism and Communion are special because Jesus told us to do them. Mention that we call these two *sacraments*. Write the word for all to see.

Reinforcing the learning

Distribute Leaflet 1 to the students. Explain that there will be a leaflet for each of the first four sessions. Point out "Data and Devotions" on the back page of the leaflet. Encourage the children to take responsibility for doing the research and leading their family in this brief worship.

Remind the group that God's love is the central meaning of Communion but there are many ways of talking about and experiencing that love. To learn about each other's experiences and thoughts, ask the group to open the leaflet to "The Interviews." Explain the activity. Be sure each young person is paired with an adult. When a child has two parents present, both should be involved in the interview. When most teams have finished, ask, "What did you learn from each other?" Invite both children and adults to share their responses.

If you won't be showing the videotape *At the Lord's Table*, explore the variety of meanings of Holy Communion by asking people to share several responses from question 5 in their interviews. List these on chalkboard or newsprint. See the list from the videotape on page 10 of this guide. Add some of them or your own if necessary. Don't worry, however, about getting a complete list. Not even adults can explore and grasp every possible aspect of the sacrament's meaning.

If you will be showing the videotape *At the Lord's Table*, introduce it by saying it will show some of the important meanings of Communion. Tell the group that you will ask afterwards if they can remember all eight of the "Holy Communion is . . ." statements in the video. Distribute pieces of scrap paper for notes if you wish. Tell the group to notice the repeated scene of a pastor breaking the loaf of Communion bread and that you will ask for their ideas as to why that was done.

Show the main segment of the video. (It lasts 15 minutes.) After viewing, ask the group to mention scenes they especially remember. Ask why they think the breaking of the loaf was repeatedly shown. *(There is no single right answer, but you may get ideas about the importance of the bread, the repetition of the sacrament, the distribution, and so on.)* Ask for the eight "Communion is . . ." statements and list them on the chalkboard or newsprint. The list is printed on page 10 of this guide. Inquire whether any of the same statements appeared in their interviews.

Ask the group to find out one way Martin Luther completed the statement "Holy Communion is . . ." by turning to the Holy Communion section of The Small Catechism on page 32 in their books. Direct them to Part 1.

Close this portion of the session with a comment about the amazing variety of meaning in God's simple gift of words, bread, and wine. Tell them they will keep making discoveries about God's love as long as they live.

Challenges and options

The section "Stretch" on page 7 of the communicant book is intended as a challenge or reinforcement activity. Ask the child/adult teams to work independently or in small groups. Discuss the answers they suggest. Answers follow.

Four things Jesus did to show love are: welcomed them, spoke to them about the kingdom of God, healed those who needed it, and fed the people. (If people need a hint, tell them to find three answers in verse 11 and one in verses 16-17.)

Many Bible students think that feeding the people is told about in a way that reminds us of Holy Communion. Note that the verbs in the phrases "*took* the five loaves," "*thanked* God for them," "*broke* them," and "*gave* them . . . to the people" (Luke 9:15-16) sound very much like the account of the last supper (Luke 22:19). Any of the other three answers could also be connected with Holy Communion—Jesus welcomes us to the meal; the meal makes God's kingdom present and real for us; Communion can offer healing of our sinful lives.

If there is extra time, have the students do the crossword puzzle "The Lord's Supper" on page 1 of the leaflet. Answers follow.

Across: *1. Baptism, 3. pews, 4. words, 5. God, 6. Communion, 7. wine, 8. love, 9. pastor.*

Down: *1. bread, 2. sacraments, 3. physical.*

"Old Words/New Words" on page 8 of the communicant book can be used as a summary by asking students to suggest which word they would pick to explain what they've learned this session.

Closing

Distribute cards or half sheets of paper and ask the parents and children to write down any questions they have, including questions they wrote down during their mutual interviews. Collect the questions and promise to deal with them in future sessions.

Have students write their name on their book and hand them in. Explain that the books can be taken home after the final session. Remind them to take the leaflet home and use the "Data and Devotions" section.

Ask someone to read aloud "Look Ahead" on page 8 of the communicant book. The next session will focus on Holy Communion as remembering Jesus' death.

Close by reading together the caption for the art on page 3 of the communicant book and John 3:16 as printed under "Focus" on page 5 of book.

Take a few minutes to explain the schedule for the rest of the course. (A printed schedule would be helpful.)

If you plan to do the session for parents as part of this gathering, excuse the young people for recreation and refreshments. Ask the parents to pick up their refreshments and return for another half hour.

Session 2: Remembering Jesus and his death

Overview

This session explores the importance of remembering Jesus and his death. It shows how remembering is important in Holy Communion and how Jesus is really present with us and for us in this meal.

Objectives

This session will help children:

- ▶ learn how the remembered words and actions in Holy Communion point to Jesus' death for our good;
- ▶ realize that the words, bread, and wine can make Jesus real and present to them;
- ▶ interview an older adult about his or her understanding of early Communion memories of church.

Materials needed

- ■ *General materials:* communicant books, leaflets for Session 2, pencils, Bibles, copies of *Lutheran Book of Worship*, chalkboard and chalk or newsprint and markers

Session background

Both the Old Testament and New Testament are filled with memories preserved by the people of God. With the

exception of the New Testament letters, most of the Bible was passed on orally before it was written down. God's people needed to remember what they and their ancestors had learned about God and about living as the people of God. These collective memories did much to establish their identity. The stories told them who they were and helped them make sense of their experiences.

The memories passed down about Jesus' last meal with his disciples are like all those other memories, and yet they were different because they were acted out. Jesus told his friends to remember him by doing what was done at that final meal. The bread and wine of that night were shared again and again. As Jesus had promised, the people discovered that Jesus was present for them in the meal. Jesus wasn't simply a figure from the past like Moses or Elijah. The earthly Jesus made God's love real, and the bread and wine of Holy Communion still make that love real. Thus Luther could say that Christ is really present "in, with, and under" the bread and wine of the Lord's Supper.

Abstract ideas of the real presence are beyond children at this age. An emphasis on the strength of memory and the effects of the meal will lay a foundation for later understanding.

Before the session

Contact any parents and children whose absences at the first session were unexplained. Try to arrange a time to visit with them.

Study the session objectives and determine how you will choose activities to meet them in the time available to you. Be sure to keep all three objectives in mind.

If you'll be visiting the worship area, place water in the baptismal font.

SESSION PLAN

Opening

Welcome students again. If there are any parents present, make them feel welcome as well. As people arrive, greet them by name and ask informally what they learned about their own Baptisms (from "Data and Devotions" on page 4 of Leaflet 1).

For an opening devotion, read the Words of Institution in the form usually used in your congregation (for example, *LBW* p. 69, rubric 32).

Use the following post-communion prayer or compose your own.

Almighty God, you gave your Son both as a sacrifice for sin and a model of the godly life. Enable us to receive him always with thanksgiving, and to conform our lives to his; through the same Jesus Christ our Lord. Amen.

As you distribute the communicant books, ask questions as review and foundation for this session. For example, say, "Last session we talked about the central meaning of Holy Communion. Who can tell what it is? *(God's love for us.)* We talked about how that love comes to us in words, bread, and wine. We also thought of several ways to finish the sentence 'Holy Communion is . . .' Who can remember some of the ways? (*One important way to finish the sentence is 'Holy Communion is remembering.')* We'll talk today about remembering Jesus' death as a reminder of God's love for us."

Ask each person to remember a very special meal of which they were a part. Give the students time to think and then ask what made that meal special. *(Answers might include the people present, the reason for the meal, the food, or what was said.)* Share a memory of your own, too. Tell the students that today they will be finding out what people thought was special and worth remembering about Jesus' last meal with his disciples.

Learning the main ideas

Introduce the story "Remembering Grandma" on page 10 of the communicant book by reminding the group that the words and the bread and wine in Holy Communion work together to make God's love real. Tell them you are going to read a story about how words and physical things helped someone remember. Read the story aloud as the students follow along.

After reading ask, "Why do you think Sara and her mom felt like they knew grandma better after that day?" If necessary, prompt their thinking by asking, "Did the 'memory table' help? Did the stories about Grandma's life help?" Summarize by reminding the students that people can share memories with us that help make the past real. If parents are present, ask for a story they have been told from their own parents' past that seems real to them, though they weren't there when it happened.

The section "Focus" on page 10 of the communicant book links the story "Remembering Grandma" to the biblical account of the last supper. Ask the students to work individually to read the section and answer the questions. Invite them to share their responses with the group.

Jesus told the disciples to eat the bread (his body) and drink the wine (his blood).

Remembering with words and physical things made Sara's grandma seem real. Words and the bread and wine of Communion make Jesus real.

Ask for volunteers to read "Get the Point" on page 11 of the communicant book. Stop and read Mark 14:22-25 at the point indicated. Ask if the words from Mark sound familiar. Point out that they are close to the words just read from 1 Corinthians 11:23-25 (see "Focus") and those used at every Communion service.

Ask the students to keep their Bibles open to Mark 14 while someone continues reading in the communicant book. Students can write in the answers to the two questions.

"Take it, this is my body."

"This is my blood which is poured out for many, my blood which seals God's covenant."

Before reading on, ask the students why they think these words are repeated to every person who communes. Direct them to the next paragraphs for an answer and continue having the paragraphs read aloud. Afterwards ask, "Do you have any questions about the bread, wine, and the words that make Jesus real to people?" Answer their questions according to your own understanding. Be careful not to get too abstract or detailed. Don't be afraid to say you don't know the answer. If that is the case, promise to try to answer the question in the next session.

Reinforcing the learning

Distribute Leaflet 2 and ask the students to turn to "The Jerusalem Journal" in the center. Read aloud the opening paragraph and give the students time to write their articles. Invite them to read their work when completed.

Then read aloud the rest of this section in the leaflet. Work together to complete the message and read it together.

Do the "Memory Joggers' Tour" on the front of the leaflet. Ask the students to bring their leaflets and pencils and move to your congregation's worship space. (If this is not possible, take them on a mental tour by asking them to close their eyes and picture the space, its furniture, and decorations.)

1. Ask the group first to move around, looking for things they see that remind them of Jesus. *(Look for crosses, pictures, stained glass, symbols.)* They can make notes in their leaflets. Gather the students together to share what they found.

2. Ask the students to imagine that they are at a Sunday worship service. What would they hear that could remind them of Jesus? Have them write their ideas in their leaflets. *(They may think of Bible texts, hymns, sermon, liturgy.)*

3. Ask what actions they could see in worship that could remind them of Jesus. Again, the students can make notes in their leaflets. *(They might suggest the serving of bread and wine, sign of the cross, exchange of peace.)*

If your congregation uses *Lutheran Book of Worship*, ask students to turn to the Brief Order for Confession and Forgiveness (pp. 56, 77, 98) and read the first rubric (the direction printed in red). Ask why the cross is a reminder of Baptism. To find the answer, ask the students to turn to the service for Holy Baptism and read rubric 14 on page page 124. *(Each person baptized receives the sign of the cross on the forehead. There also is a deeper answer to the question. Mention it if parents are present, but it's probably too abstract and symbolic for children this age. Paul reminds us in Romans 6:3-4 that when we were baptized, we were joined with Christ in death so that we might also live with Christ.)*

4. While still seated in the worship area, ask the young people ways in which Holy Communion makes Jesus' death real to us. *(Bread/body, wine/blood as pointing to his death; the sign of the cross; the timing—the night he was betrayed; the reminder of forgiveness that comes*

through his death). Ask someone to read 1 Corinthians 11:26. Then ask each student to write down which reminder makes Jesus most real to him or her. Invite the students to share their answers with the group. Share your answer too.

Challenges and options

If you do "Stretch" on page 13 of the communicant book, the comparison of texts does not need to be done in great detail. Comparing any two will indicate that the wording does not quite agree. There also are slight differences of order. Nevertheless, all suggest the importance of this event for Christians and how it relates to Jesus' death. Despite the differences in wording, all link the bread and cup of wine with Jesus' body and blood.

"Old Words/New Words" on page 14 of the communicant book can be used for review. You could ask the students to identify which word helps them explain what they learned in this session. Or, ask the students to review the section silently while you list the words on the chalkboard or newsprint. Then ask volunteers to give definitions in their own words (with books closed).

If there is extra time, have the group look through *Lutheran Book of Worship* (hymns 196-226) for hymns that help them remember Jesus and the last supper. You might sing one verse together.

Closing

Remind the young people about doing "Data and Devotions" on the back of the leaflet.

Ask a volunteer to read "Look Ahead" on page 14 of the communicant book.

If you are still in the worship area, gather everyone around the baptismal font. Remind the students about the sign of the cross that was made on their foreheads at Baptism. Tell them the cross is the most powerful sign of God's love for each of them. Dip your finger in water and trace the sign of the cross on your own forehead. Invite them to do the same, in remembrance of their Baptism.

Session 3: A meal shared with many

Overview

This session explores how the Lord's Supper unites us with God and with all of God's people. The phrase "communion of saints" from the Apostles' Creed and the links to the Old Testament people will be studied.

Objectives

This session will help children:

- understand that Communion unites us with all Christians, with all people who trust God;
- experience a sense of Christian community, of belonging within the class group;
- find a way to express community by sharing.

Materials needed

- *General materials:* communicant books, leaflets for Session 3, pencils, Bibles, copies of *Lutheran Book of Worship*
- *Learning the main ideas:* portable communion kit, copies of Luther's Small Catechism (optional)
- *Reinforcing the learning:* your congregation's communion ware
- *Closing:* a simple treat (cake, pizza, loaf of cinnamon bread—something to cut and share); newsletters, bulletins, brochures, or annual reports that mention ways your congregation serves others

Session background

In the Apostles' Creed, the phrase "communion of saints" is not a direct reference to Holy Communion. However, it points to an important fact about Holy Communion. Through that meal, we are united with all the saints. Saints are those whom God has called to lives of faith. We are united with all the baptized people of God in every time and every place. All people who trust God are one family or community. This is God's doing, not ours. We enjoy God-given community. Thus our true community survives even when we deny or ignore it by our actions.

The basis for our communion with all God's saints is our communion with God. Through Christ we are drawn into fellowship with God. We are justified. Communion makes Jesus real for us. It makes God's love real for us, as God intends it to be. That creates faith, and that's the relationship that exists between us and God—God loves us and we trust God.

Before the session

Arrange for a pianist if you want accompaniment for the hymn during "Opening."

Arrange for students (or a parent) to read the opening story if you wish.

Have the congregation's normal Holy Communion ware set out on the altar (or on a table in the class areas if you will be unable to use the worship area).

SESSION PLAN

Opening

Gather the class in a circle, standing or sitting. Pass out copies of *Lutheran Book of Worship*.

Begin by asking a volunteer to read 1 Corinthians 10:16-17. Then sing or read the words to "Let Us Break Bread Together" (*LBW* 212). Lay down the books, join hands, and pray the Lord's Prayer together. Introduce the prayer by reminding the group that our most familiar prayer begins "*Our* Father," not "*My* Father," because trust in God as loving parent is something we share with many others.

Learning the main ideas

Read the story "The Great Circle" on page 16 of the communicant book or have it read by volunteers. After the story has been read, invite students to tell you in their own words about Ricardo's dream. Ask, "Have you heard of the Apostles' Creed? Do you know when we all say it together? Why do you think Ricardo's mother thought about the Creed?" Accept whatever answers they give to the last question—or no answer. Tell them they will find out more later.

Ask the students to work individually to complete "Focus" on page 17 of the communicant book. Invite them to share their responses.

"We" in 1 Corinthians 10:16-17 originally meant Paul and the Corinthian Christians to whom he wrote. However, we can read his statement to include all who receive the Lord's Supper.

Some students may have answered "no" to the question about being included, since they don't yet receive Communion. If they answered no, assure them that they do belong to the one body since God's love is for all. Tell them that receiving Communion is strong evidence of that.

Assure the students that all of the people in Ricardo's dream belong to the body of Christ. This includes people of every time and place.

God's people are united or one because God in Christ makes us one.

If you have extra time, explain that Paul was writing to Christians like ourselves who sometimes behaved selfishly, forgetting that they were all one. Paul tried to help them remember. Ask for suggestions of good ways Christians can show their oneness. (*Working together, caring about each other, forgiving each other.*) Be prepared to mention specific things in and beyond your congregation that affirm oneness.

Move on to "Get the Point" on page 17 of the communicant book. Ask volunteers to take turns reading aloud. Tell them in advance that you will be stopping after some paragraphs to talk.

After the first paragraph, show them a portable Communion kit and explain that it is used because even people who can't come to church are in union with God and other Christians. Holy Communion helps keep them confident of their links to God and other believers. Receiving Communion is often very important and helpful for these people.

After the second paragraph, ask the students if they understand why Ricardo's mother might have thought of the Apostles' Creed. *(It's something that unites us with other Christians and it refers to "the communion of saints.")* Be sure they understand that "communion" in that phrase means unity or community and doesn't refer explicitly to the Lord's Supper. If you have ready access to copies of Luther's Small Catechism, have the students look at the explanation of the Third Article of the Creed. Have them find the themes of unity with Christ and being gathered together.

Continue reading up to the paragraph that begins "The sacrifices offered at the temple. . . ." Then explain that God's love had been shown and known to people for thousands of years before Jesus came. Help them see that the Old Testament is like a foundation for our understanding of what it means to be the people of God. We are linked with other people of God, even though they do not share in the Lord's Supper with us. The Lord's Supper still points us to God's love for all people. The circle of God's love is very large.

Make the positive point of God's love for all. Don't worry in this session about making the necessary distinctions between Christians and Jews. It is important here to affirm our Christian unity and to remember that we are not a closed circle or an exclusive club.

Have students read the final two paragraphs.

Reinforcing the learning

To help the students think about the theme of unity (and provide them with time for some movement), tell them they are going on another tour of your worship space. Last time they were looking for reminders of Jesus and his death. This time they are to be artists, architects, and worship planners who are trying to help people experience Christian community. They will be trying to identify things that express our unity with God and our unity with one another.

Move to your worship area and let the group walk and look around. Students could do this activity in pairs. Begin by looking for things that can be seen, then have them remember what happens in worship. If necessary, remind them of things that might express unity of either sort. *(Gathering at the altar shows both aspects of the unity. A circular altar rail suggests links to other Christians, as may memorials present in the worship area. Think also of what happens there—gathering, praying, and singing praise together.)*

After talking about what presently exists in your worship and worship space, move on to talk about possible improvements. Be seated so you can see each other. If the class is large, divide it into groups of five to six. Have the students imagine they are architects, artists, or members of the congregation's worship committee. Ask each group to come up with new ideas to express our unity with God, with other members of the congregation, and with all people. Tell them they can think about moving pews or the altar, adding windows or art work, or doing something new in worship. Encourage original thinking. If there are several groups, go from one to another to hear what they are discussing. Then have the groups share ideas with each other.

This could be a good time to sample the bread and wine used in Holy Communion and see the congregation's Communion ware. The pastor should be present. This activity also could be done in Session 4 or 5. Gather the group around the altar. Remind students how Communion is served in your congregation. Point to the bread (or wafers) and wine. Remind them that no matter how Communion is served, the bread and wine are the means to unite us to God and to bring us together. Tell them you want them to sample both the bread and the wine so that they will know what to expect. Explain and demonstrate how the bread and wine are served in your congregation. Encourage them to sip the wine slowly and tell them it is not necessary to drink every drop. Expect some giggling and silly comments. That is part of the way kids deal with what is unfamiliar. When all have sampled the bread and wine, ask them if they think that it was Holy Communion that they just had. *(It wasn't, because it wasn't done to remember Christ but rather simply to let them taste the elements. The promises of God weren't included.)*

Return to the class area if convenient. Distribute Leaflet 3 and have the students turn to "Living Our Unity" in the center. Explain that the questions are to help them think what it means for them, at their age, to live as part of God's community. Allow several minutes for writing.

When most students have finished, invite them to share their responses. Remind them that Christians don't think only of other *Christians*. The unity of the church is a unity in mission, a unity in service. Ask them how, together, they could serve people beyond the congregation. Have some project ideas in mind (pick up litter in a nearby park or public area, visit a nursing home, collect food for a community food shelf). Help them pick a project and say, "Let's do it." Make necessary plans to carry out the project during or before your next session. Follow up with calls or letters if you need to let parents know the plans.

Challenges and options

Introduce "Stretch" on page 19 of the communicant book by reading the first sentence to the class. Stop and ask if the students can think of cases where Christians forget that they are really one community of love (local disagreements or hatred between Christians or issues mentioned in the news). Then have them work on this activity in groups of two or three. Discuss their responses. Suggestions for discussion follow.

The problem mentioned in verse 18 is that there were opposing groups among the Corinthian Christians.

Paul says that some of the people ate and drank in excess, rather than eating together in the spirit of the Lord's Supper. Some were hungry while others ate too much.

Paul said they were not eating together in the way the Lord's Supper should be celebrated.

Let the students give examples of ways Christians forget their unity.

"Old Words/New Words" on page 20 of the communicant book can be used for review. Encourage the students to discuss and ask questions about any words that are unclear.

Ask the students to turn to "Prayers of Intercession" on the front page of Leaflet 3. Explain that these prayers are about the needs of others. Read this section aloud. Ask for examples of persons or groups for whom they might want to intercede. Perhaps the intercessory prayers the students write could be printed in your Sunday bulletin for use by the congregation. Tell the students you will invite them to pray their prayers as part of the closing.

If there is time, have the group study John 6:28-35. This passage talks about Jesus as the bread of life. Compare its themes with the first stanzas of *LBW* hymns 197 ("O Living Bread from Heaven") and 222 ("O Bread of Life from Heaven"). Ask students which hymn seems to them to be more directly based on John 6.

You also could look up the Old Testament passages referred to in "Get the Point" and have them read aloud or invite early finishers to do this.

Closing

Take a few minutes to pray the intercessory prayers the students wrote. Be sure to ask for volunteers.

Have one of the students read "Look Ahead" on page 20 of the communicant book. Remind them of the time of the next session.

Surprise the class with a simple treat such as a pizza, a cake, or loaf of cinnamon bread—something that can be cut and shared as a reminder of our unity. Or have a pitcher of juice and have each person pour a glass for someone else. This could be done by going around the circle, each one pouring for the person on the left.

Point out the "Data and Devotions" project on the back of the leaflet and give them any resource pieces they need such as photocopies of church bulletins and newsletters. Be sure the copies contain fairly obvious references to what the congregation does for others. Encourage them also to ask people for more examples. Remind the young people to lead devotions for their family.

Session 4: Forgiveness is life

Overview

This session will explore the benefits of the Lord's Supper, focusing on those Luther mentions in the Catechism—forgiveness of sins, life, and salvation.

Objectives

This session will help children:

- understand several aspects of forgiveness through Holy Communion;
- experience forgiveness, acceptance, and belonging;
- contribute to an experience of forgiveness and acceptance for others.

Materials needed

- *General materials:* communicant books, leaflets for Session 4, pencils, Bibles, copies of *Lutheran Book of Worship*, chalkboard and chalk or newsprint and markers
- *Reinforcing the learning:* note cards or small sheets of paper, plain envelopes
- *Challenges and options:* collage materials (optional)—magazines and newspapers, tagboard, glue or paste, scissors, black marker

Session background

Forgiveness is one of the best descriptions of God's gift because it is a term we readily understand and because we see the benefits of forgiveness in everyday life. However, it is only one of several important biblical words for describing the relationship that we have with God through Christ.

Covenant is a word with a history that stretches back to the stories of Noah and Abraham. God established with Israel a relationship of promise and expectation. God also provided means for keeping that covenant strong. In Baptism, God establishes a covenant with us. The Lord's Supper is a way of renewing and strengthening that covenant.

Trust is at the basis of all the ways of understanding God's gift. God creates trust in people by loving them. Without trust, we could not even accept the forgiveness God offers. Although Luther doesn't mention it in The Small Catechism, he often stressed that the Lord's Supper is meant to strengthen our trust.

Before the session

Review the material and decide which activities you will choose to meet the session's objectives.

Choose two students to read the dialog on page 22 of the communicant book.

SESSION PLAN

Opening

Read Matthew 6:14-15.

Use the confession in the right-hand column from Prayer at the Close of the Day (*LBW* p. 155). Have half the class read the "L" part and half the "C" part. You can read with one of the groups. If parents are present, ask adults to read "L" and students "C."

Learning the main ideas

Remind the group that in the last session you talked about community with God and others through Holy Communion. Tell them this session focuses on one thing that helps restore our community with God and people—forgiveness.

Ask for two volunteers to read the dialog "Forgiving and Living" on page 22 of the communicant book. If possible, let them have a few minutes to look it over before they begin.

After the dialog has been read, encourage discussion by asking, "Have any of you had experiences like Meg and her friends? How does it feel to be angry at a friend? How does it feel to make up and be friends again? Did going out for pizza help make the forgiveness in the story real? How do you and your friends handle problems that arise?"

You may wish to talk also about forgiveness between youth and adults. If so, be sure you look at both sides!

Work together through "Focus" on page 22 of the communicant book. Encourage the students to discuss their responses; accept all answers. Answers will vary.

Ask the students to look back at the title of the dialog on page 22 of their books. Why do they think that title was chosen?

Ask the students to turn to "Old Words/New Words" on page 25 of the communicant book. Have a volunteer read the definitions of *benefit* and *remission*. Then turn to "The Sacrament of Holy Communion" on page 32 of the communicant book and find Part 2. Ask one person to read the question and another to read Luther's answer. Have the class find the words that Luther uses to describe the benefits of Communion. *(Remission of sins, forgiveness of sins, life, salvation.)* Write them on the chalkboard or newsprint as they are given.

Have two more students read the question and answer in Part 3. On the chalkboard or newsprint write, *words (promises) + bread + wine = forgiveness from God.* Say, "God makes forgiveness real to us through bread, wine, and words of promise." Remind them of the opening dialog and ask how this statement is like Meg and her friends going out for pizza. *(The meal is evidence of the forgiveness and strengthens the experience of being forgiven.)*

Introduce "Get the Point" on page 23 of the communicant book by telling the students they're going to read about different ways of describing the gifts God gives us in Communion. After you have read about each gift, stop and ask the students to underline an important thought in each paragraph. Discuss reasons for their choices. Ask which way of describing God's gift they find most helpful.

Reinforcing the learning

Read aloud the caption under the art on page 21 of

the communicant book. Distribute Leaflet 4 to the students and give them time to do the word find on the front of the leaflet. A completed word find follows.

E	E	N	O	I	T	A	I	L	I	C	N	O	C	E	R	L
H	F	R	A	G	A	U	T	T	G	S	F	L	E	E	S	A
M	I	O	I	R	V	G	O	D	I	F	I	V	R	C	G	T
Y	L	N	R	B	T	L	P	M	F	R	E	E	D	O	M	G
A	F	O	L	G	W	M	A	R	T	L	P	N	O	N	R	F
D	L	D	F	A	I	T	H	O	B	X	O	D	K	P	A	F
C	B	Q	O	G	L	V	M	Y	L	O	H	E	J	I	S	B
R	S	E	V	C	C	M	E	N	C	M	Y	L	I	O	N	L
C	O	M	M	U	N	I	O	N	M	F	P	H	A	R	B	P
Q	J	N	T	U	A	O	B	V	E	G	C	Z	Q	A	Y	A
L	M	N	O	I	T	A	V	L	A	S	F	B	I	M	F	B
H	N	F	H	A	S	E	L	L	R	T	S	Z	M	I	K	F
O	G	J	U	S	T	I	F	I	C	A	T	I	O	N	U	B

Take some time to write notes of confession and forgiveness. Seat students far enough apart so that they can write in privacy. Distribute the note cards or paper and envelopes. Tell the students to think of people they need to forgive and people whose forgiveness they need. Ask them to write either a note of confession asking for forgiveness, or a note of forgiveness telling someone that they want to be friends again. Give examples of both kinds of note. (They can write more than one.)

Suggest that this should be a very quiet time so that all of the group can think. You should also write a note. Have the students put their notes in the envelopes, seal them, and put on the outside the name of the person to whom they wrote. Encourage them to deliver the note or to speak their confession or forgiveness to that person. Tell them that the power of God's love can help them forgive and accept forgiveness.

As an alternative or addition to this project, do "A Confession Prayer" in the center of Leaflet 4. Look together at the Brief Order for Confession and Forgiveness, (*LBW* p. 56). Point to the presider's third sentence, "If we say. . . ." Ask students what that verse says about us and about God. *(We are sinners. God will forgive.)* Then direct students to the bold print prayer of confession and have them proceed individually. Invite them to share prayers.

Challenges and options

Encourage students to write a story as suggested under "A Forgiveness Story" in the center of Leaflet 4. This can be done in class or at home. Suggest that the story should help us better understand what forgiveness is and does. You could give them the option of creating a cartoon strip to illustrate forgiveness.

Ask the students to work in teams of two on "Stretch" on page 25 of the communicant book. Each team should look at all the verses. Suggestions for discussion follow.

Romans 4:7-8 *They are happy (blessed).*

Romans 5:1-2 *We are put right (justified). We have peace, grace, and hope.*

Roman 5:8-10 *Jesus' death changes us from God's enemies into friends and saves us.*

1 John 1:9 *God will forgive us and purify (cleanse) us.*

As in previous sessions, you could use "Old Words/New Words" for review. They are on page 25 in the communicant book.

Make a forgiveness collage. Supply old magazines and newspapers. Have students (and parents) look for words or pictures that show a need for forgiveness and glue them to tagboard to make a collage. When the glue has dried, have each student write "forgiven" across the page with a black marker.

Closing

Ask someone to read "Look Ahead" on page 25 of the communicant book.

Remind the students to continue using "Data and Devotions" from the back page of their leaflets.

Make an "acceptance circle." Gather the group in a circle and have them hold hands. Tell them that feeling accepted is part of being forgiven. We are all accepted and forgiven by God, but sometimes people are not very accepting. We're not kind to everyone, and it really hurts to feel rejected. Ask the group to think silently of times they've felt rejected, and then of times they've enjoyed acceptance. Join hands. Then in turn say each person's name. After you say a name, everyone else responds by saying, "We're glad you're here!" Squeeze hands and let go.

Session 5: Trusting and ready

Overview

Luther says that one is properly prepared and worthy for Communion when one believes the words "for you." This session explores the meaning of trust and leads young people to express their trust in the God who creates trust in us.

Objectives

This session will help children:

- learn that trust indicates worthiness and readiness for Holy Communion, and that Communion creates and strengthens trust;
- deepen their faith in God who gives love through this meal;
- decide, in conversation with parent(s), whether this is an appropriate time to begin receiving Communion.

This session will help parents:

- learn that trust indicates worthiness and readiness for Holy Communion, and that Communion creates and strengthens trust;
- deepen their faith in God who gives love through this meal;
- support the young person in making his or her own decision.

Materials needed

- *General materials:* communicant books, pencils, Bibles, copies of *Lutheran Book of Worship*, chalkboard and chalk or newsprint and markers
- *Learning the main ideas:* videotape *At the Lord's Table* and equipment for showing the video (optional)

Session background

From the beginning, Christians have struggled to keep a strong emphasis on God's grace without making people seem like puppets. The Bible holds together an undeniable assertion that salvation is entirely God's gift and a clear sense that people will accept that gift. The key to this tension is trust. Trust is not something we add to God's gift, but without trust we do not receive the benefits of the gift. God's love draws trust from us.

At this point of deciding whether to begin receiving Communion, the young people, the parents, and the leaders should keep the emphasis on gift and grace. Proclamation of God's love has been a theme of this course because that is God's own way to create saving faith. If you have misgivings about the readiness of some of your students, remember also that the sacrament itself creates and strengthens faith.

Before the session

If the pastor has not been leading these sessions, it would be very helpful to have her or him present for this final session. You may wish to ask the pastor to lead the segment where you consider the Holy Communion service from *Lutheran Book of Worship*. He or she could use the suggested activity or handle it another way. Be sure to be clear about the amount of time you have alotted for that and explain the objectives for the session.

If you will be choosing Communion hymns (see "Challenges and Options" on page 51) arrange to have a pianist.

SESSION PLAN

Opening

Use the opening dialog from the Great Thanksgiving (*LBW* pp. 68, 88, 109). Conclude with this prayer.

It is indeed right and helpful to praise and thank you, our loving God. Thank you for these young people and their parents. We praise you for the time we have had to learn together about your love and your gifts to us. Guide each of us in preparing for Holy Communion. Help us trust you. Amen.

Learning the main ideas

Move directly into the story "Trust—20 Feet Up" on page 27 of the communicant book. Ask the group to follow along as you read. Ask afterward, "How do you think you would have felt up on that cable? Why? Why did the counselor tell Mitch he was ready if he trusted the equipment?" Then ask, "What *things* do you have to trust in daily life? *(Floors, stairs, elevators, rain coats, cars, and so forth.)* What people do you have to trust? *(Parents, friends, teachers, government officials, bus drivers, salespeople, and so forth.)"*

Introduce "Focus" on page 28 of the communicant book by saying, "We trust God and we trust Christ's promises given with bread and wine." Have each child/adult team work together to read this section and answer the questions as they go along. When most are finished, ask what Luther said is most important in being prepared for Communion. *(Believing.)*

Answer the last two questions as a group.

Mitch would have missed the fun.

We would miss the love of God available to us in the Lord's Supper.

Remind students and parents that these sessions have tried to bring participants to a deeper understanding and appreciation of the Lord's Supper. Out of that appreciation can come stronger trust in God.

For some or all of the children, it also has been a time to move toward a decision about beginning to receive Communion. Tell them there is really only one question to ask oneself about being ready—"Do I trust the promise that the benefits of Communion are meant for me?"

Ask everyone to turn to the portion of Luther's Small Catechism printed on page 32 of the communicant book and page 32 of the parent book. Ask a parent to read the question in Part 4 and ask a student to read the answer. Point out Luther's emphasis on *believing* for being prepared to receive Communion. Luther wasn't talking only about people coming to Communion for the first time. Trust is all that's asked of us the first time and every time we receive.

Ask for volunteers to read "Get the Point" on page 29 of the communicant book. Stop after the third paragraph and the fifth one and have them read again for emphasis.

Reinforcing the learning

Worship can strengthen and express our trust. Spend some time looking at the service normally used for Holy Communion in your congregation. Point out the two movements of worship—from God to us (blessings, good news to strengthen faith) and from us to God (thanks and praise that express God-given faith).

Make three columns on the chalkboard or newsprint as shown below. Look at the various parts of the service and ask the group to place them in the correct column. There may be some disagreement, and exact divisions are not important. The point is to see that both movements are present and that the love of God creates movements.

Faith strengthening	**Both or either**	**Faith expressing**
Forgiveness	Kyrie	Confession
Lessons	Prayer of the Day	Hymn of Praise
Gospel	Sermon	Creed
Words of Institution	Eucharistic Prayer	Offering
Bread and wine	Hymns	Great Thanksgiving
Benediction	Anthems	Rubric 36 ("Amen")
Dismissal		

Seeing the videotape *At the Lord's Table* would be a good way to review. An option would be to look over the first page of each session in the communicant book. Read the titles for the sessions and also the captions under the illustrations.

Challenges and options

Do "Stretch" on page 31 of the communicant book by working in groups of about six. Ask the groups also to review the words under "Old Words/New Words."

Have the students and adults write prayers that would help them prepare for receiving Communion. Could these prayers be printed in the worship bulletin for the next Communion service?

If most of the young people will be receiving their first Communion the same Sunday, try to get permission to let them choose Communion hymns (*LBW* 196-226) to be sung during distribution. Arrange for a pianist so that they can hear how they sound, but encourage them to look first at the words.

If the students have not seen the congregation's communion ware, do so now and let them sample the bread and wine used. (See notes under "Reinforcing the Learning" on page 36 of this guide for additional suggestions.)

Closing

The pastor should again issue an invitation to begin receiving the Lord's Supper. Encourage conversation at home and offer to talk with anyone who has more questions or concerns. Mention when Holy Communion will be celebrated. Make any necessary announcements.

Sing together "Come, Let Us Eat," (*LBW* 214) or another Communion hymn that is essentially an invitation. Close with, "Go in peace, serve the Lord." The group may respond, "Thanks be to God."

Session for parents only

Session for parents only

This session will help parents:

- ▶ obtain answers to questions and concerns they might not raise with children present;
- ▶ feel that first Communion readiness should be approached in terms of God's gifts, not God's demands;
- ▶ make a commitment to learning together with their child.

Materials needed

- ■ *General materials:* parent books and refreshments

Before the session

If the pastor is not teaching the course, invite her or him to be present for this session.

If this session immediately follows Session 1, have parents pick up their own refreshments; they need to stretch. When all have been served, ask them to be seated again.

SESSION PLAN

Opening

Begin by thanking the parents and other adults for their presence and support in this important part of the confirmation ministry of your congregation. Suggest that this session for parents can be fairly brief, but that you want to be sure they understand the plans and receive answers for any questions they have. Take a few minutes to explain the appropriateness of teaching children of this age about Holy Communion and how helpful it is for parents to learn along with the children.

If it has been less than five years since your congregation lowered the age for first Communion or separated it from confirmation, it is probably necessary to review the reasons for that decision. Some parents may not have paid much attention to the discussions at the time, especially if their own children were still very young. Allow for questions and comments. Don't be defensive if some parents object to the new policies. Share your personal convictions and the positive experience of many. Encourage them to remain open for the present, but also tell them that finally the decision about a child beginning Communion rests with the parents, the child, and the church. For each child it is to be a guided, but individual, decision. Explain that these instructional sessions are offered as a resource to help parent and child make the decision.

Emphasis on grace and faith

In your own words, explain that you want to maintain an emphasis throughout the program on God's love, using this as an opportunity to proclaim the good news about Jesus. Although it is important that we all grow in understanding, there is no knowledge test that can say a person is worthy of Communion.

Distribute the parent books and ask the participants to turn to the Holy Communion portion of the Small Catechism on page 32. Ask someone to read Part 4 aloud. Emphasize the idea that the gift of faith is what is needed to be prepared to receive Communion. Tell the parents your most important objective is to help each of their children really believe those words "for you." Ask the parents to work with you to keep the emphasis on love and not on demands for minimum knowledge or specific behavior. Encourage them to think and talk of Holy Communion as God's gift and not as a reward for anything we have done.

Ask for questions or comments. Allow plenty of time. Discussion may get off to a slow start, but be patient.

Explain the program

Ask parents to turn to "Table of Contents" on page 2 in the parent book. Briefly give a summary of the book's content. Have participants turn to "Introduction" on page 3 and follow along as you read this section aloud. As an option, you could summarize the information for them. Explain, too, the information presented in "About the Course" on page 4. Ask parents to take the book home and read the material as their children are progressing through the course.

Be explicit about the parent's need to help the child make a decision about beginning to receive Communion. Suggest when in the program this is appropriate and when Communion services are scheduled. Ask for questions.

If there is time and interest, spend some time on the section "Questions Children (and Parents) May Ask" on page 20.

Review specific expectations you have of the parents:

- attendance at joint sessions;
- getting children to their sessions;
- time for conversation with their child;
- support for the "Data and Devotions" project;
- contact you with questions or problems.

Ask parents to think right now about times that would work well for informal conversations and for the devotions. Remind them that the child is to take the lead in the devotions period but that they can provide encouragement.

Close by asking once more for questions. Thank parents and other adults again for their interest and cooperation.

The Sacrament of Holy Communion

1 What is Holy Communion?

Holy Communion is the body and blood of our Lord Jesus Christ given with bread and wine, instituted by Christ himself for us to eat and drink.

Where do the Scriptures say this?

Matthew, Mark, Luke, and Paul say:

Our Lord Jesus Christ, in the night in which he was betrayed,
took bread; and when he had given thanks,
he broke it and gave it to his disciples,
saying, "Take, eat, this is my body,
which is given for you;
this do in remembrance of me."

After the same manner also he took the cup after supper,
and when he had given thanks,
he gave it to them, saying,
"Drink of it, all of you;
this cup is the new testament in my blood,
which is shed for you, and for many, for the remission of sins:
this do, as often as you drink it, in remembrance of me."

2 What benefits do we receive from this sacrament?

The benefits of this sacrament are pointed out by the words,
given and shed for you for the remission of sins.
These words assure us that in the sacrament
we receive forgiveness of sins, life, and salvation.
For where there is forgiveness of sins,
there is also life and salvation.

3 How can eating and drinking do all this?

It is not eating and drinking that does this,
but the words, *given and shed for you for the remission of sins.*
These words, along with eating and drinking, are the main thing in the sacrament.
And whoever believes these words
has exactly what they say, forgiveness of sins.

4 When is a person rightly prepared to received this sacrament?

Fasting and other outward preparations serve a good purpose.
However, that person is well prepared and worthy who believes these words,
given and shed for you for the remission of sins.
But anyone who does not believe these words, or doubts them,
is neither prepared nor worthy,
for the words *for you* require simply a believing heart.